IT'S FOR YOU, SNOOPY

Also by the same author

and available in Coronet Books

It's for You, Snoopy

Selected Cartoons from SUNDAY'S FUN DAY, CHARLIE BROWN, Vol. 1

Charles M. Schulz

CORONET BOOKS
Hodder Fawcett Ltd., London

Printed and bound in Great Britain for
Coronet Books,
Hodder Fawcett Ltd,
St. Paul's House, Warwick Lane,
London, E.C.4
by Hazell Watson & Viney Ltd,
Aylesbury, Bucks

ISBN 0 340 15829 8

NOW I'M TOO TIRED TO EAT!

ALTHOUGH I CAN SEE WHERE HAVING TOO MANY FRIENDS COULD BE HARD ON THE STOMACH!

I'M GOING IN FOR LUNCH, SNOOPY...
HOLD THIS FOR ME...

WHATEVER YOU DO, DON'T
LET GO OF IT!

HI, THERE, TIGER!

HI, SNOOPY... HOW ARE YOU TODAY?

HELLO, SNOOPY

ORDINARILY, I FROWN ON CARD PLAYING, BUT BRIDGE IS A PRETTY GOOD GAME, AND, AFTER ALL, THEY DO NEED A PLACE TO PLAY...

"PASS"?!

SOME PEOPLE JUST SHOULDN'T PLAY CARDS TOGETHER!

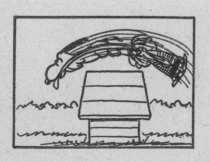

AND PAY ATTENTION TO THE BALL GAME!

PLUNK

PTUI!

I SUPPOSE IT WOULDN'T HURT TO LET HIM HAVE A LITTLE SNACK BETWEEN INNINGS...

STUPID LEAVES!

SIT UP, SNOOPY, AND
I'LL GIVE YOU A NICE
PIECE OF CANDY...

HUMPF!

"SIT UP, SNOOPY, AND I'LL
GIVE YOU A NICE PIECE OF
CANDY."...PHOOEY!
WHO NEEDS IT?!

CLOMP!

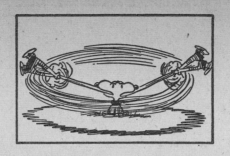

WHY WAS I LATE FOR SCHOOL TODAY? WELL, IT WAS THIS WAY...

IT'S A LIVING!

THIS IS GOING TO BE ONE OF THOSE DAYS WHEN WE GET NOTHING BUT SINGLES

ARE YOU GOING TO BUY COMIC BOOKS, CHARLIE BROWN?

NOT ON YOUR LIFE!

SEE THIS FIVE DOLLARS? I'M GOING TO SPEND IT ALL ON BUBBLE GUM CARDS! I'VE **GOT** TO GET A PICTURE OF **JOE SHLABOTNIK**!

FIVE DOLLARS' WORTH OF BUBBLE GUM, PLEASE!

I'D DO ANYTHING TO GET A JOE SHLABOTNIK BUBBLE GUM CARD.. HE'S MY HERO...

FIVE DOLLARS' WORTH OF BUBBLE GUM, AND NOT ONE JOE SHLABOTNIK!

A PENNY'S WORTH OF BUBBLE GUM, PLEASE..

WELL, WHAT DO YOU KNOW...JOE SHLABOTNIK!

PTUI!

PTUI!

UNTIL IT IS DEMONSTRATED, ONE
FORGETS THE REALLY GREAT
DIFFERENCE THAT EXISTS BETWEEN
THE MERELY COMPETENT AMATEUR
AND THE VERY EXPERT PROFESSIONAL

THERE'S THAT LITTLE RED-HAIRED GIRL WALKING HOME FROM SCHOOL...JUST THINK... I'M WALKING ON THE SAME SIDEWALK SHE'S WALKING ON

OF COURSE, I'M WALKING SEVEN BLOCKS BEHIND HER, BUT I'M WALKING ON THE VERY SAME SIDEWALK

I WISH I WERE WALKING WITH HER...I WISH I WERE WALKING RIGHT BESIDE HER, AND WE WERE TALKING

SHE WENT INTO THAT NICE HOUSE! SO THAT'S WHERE SHE LIVES...AND THERE'S THE DOOR SHE WENT IN...

I WISH SHE'D INVITE ME OVER TO HER HOUSE SOME TIME.. I WISH SHE'D COME UP TO ME, AND SAY, "WHY DON'T YOU COME OVER TO MY HOUSE AFTER SCHOOL, CHARLIE BROWN?"

THERE SHE IS AGAIN..SHE WENT INTO THE BACKYARD, AND SHE'S SWINGING ON HER SWING-SET...

WE COULD WALK HOME FROM SCHOOL TOGETHER, AND THEN WE COULD SWING ON HER SWING-SET...

BOY, WHAT A BLOCKHEAD I AM! I'LL NEVER GET TO SWING WITH HER! I'LL NEVER GET TO WALK WITH HER! I'LL NEVER EVEN GET TO SAY ONE WORD TO HER!

ALL I GET TO DO IS WALK HOME FROM SCHOOL BY MYSELF, AND....

OH, HI, SNOOPY

YOU'RE NOT MUCH OF A SUBSTITUTE FOR A LITTLE RED-HAIRED GIRL

QUITE OFTEN LATELY I HAVE THE FEELING I DON'T KNOW WHAT'S GOING ON...

Linus Van Pelt
ENGLISH I

SNOOPY, I'D LIKE TO READ YOU A STORY I'VE WRITTEN AND ILLUSTRATED FOR SCHOOL...

"ONCE THERE WAS A LITTLE GIRL WHO HAD A HEADACHE."

HER MOM GAVE HER SOME PILLS, BUT THEY DIDN'T HELP. HER MOM THEN TOOK HER TO THE DOCTOR.

"THE DOCTOR WAS UNABLE TO FIND ANYTHING WRONG."

"THIS IS A MYSTERIOUS CASE," HE SAID.

"THE LITTLE GIRL'S MOTHER TOOK HER HOME, AND PUT HER TO BED... HER HEAD THROBBED."

"HER LITTLE BROTHER CAME IN, AND SAID, 'MAYBE YOUR EARS ARE TOO TIGHT.'"

SO HE LOOSENED EACH EAR ONE TURN BACK. HER HEADACHE SUDDENLY STOPPED, AND SHE NEVER HAD ANOTHER HEADACHE AGAIN.

I GUESS HE DIDN'T LIKE IT.... THAT WAS HIS "GOOD LUCK, YOU'RE GOING TO NEED IT" HANDSHAKE!

HERE'S THE FIERCE MOUNTAIN LION WAITING FOR HIS VICTIM...

BLEAH!

WHY FREEZE TO DEATH WHEN YOU DON'T HAVE TO?

BAM BAM BAM

IF YOU THROW THAT SNOWBALL AT ME, I'LL HAVE THE HUMANE SOCIETY ON YOU SO FAST IT'LL MAKE YOUR HEAD SWIM!

WHOEVER PAINTS THOSE SIGNS FOR HIM, DOES A GOOD JOB!

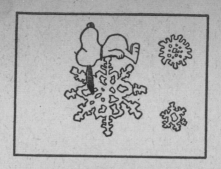

Happiness is catching
snowflakes on your tongue.

ALTHOUGH, I WILL ADMIT YOU HAVE BEEN A GOOD NEIGHBOR...YOU LOOK QUITE HANDSOME WITH YOUR COAL EYES AND CARROT NOSE..

OH, WELL, ONE CAN'T DELIBERATELY AVOID FRIENDSHIPS, I GUESS...

YOU CAN'T KEEP TO YOURSELF JUST BECAUSE YOU'RE AFRAID OF BEING HURT, OR...

AAUGH!
SOB

POOR SNOOPY...I SEE HE'S LOST ANOTHER FRIEND.. IT'S TOO BAD.... HE'S SO SENSITIVE...

UH, HUH... BUT I NOTICE HE WASN'T TOO SENSITIVE TO EAT THE CARROT!